Let's Write Fiction:

Tears, Fears, Confidence, Book

By
Rebecka Vigus

Other Books by Rebecka Vigus
Stand Alone Novels
Secrets
Out of the Flames
Target of Vengeance
Rescue Mountain

Children's

Of Moonbeams and Fairies: Collected Tales
G is for Gymnastics
Santa is for Real

Macy McVannel Series

Rivers Edge
Crossing the Line
Sanctuary
Something Borrowed, Something Blue

Poetry

Only a Start and Beyond

Self-Help

So You Think You Want to be a Mommy?

Collections

Damsels Distressed

Copyright © 2022 Rebecka Vigus

All rights reserved under the Copyright Act of 1976, no part of this book shall be reproduced or transmitted in any form or by any means; electronic, mechanical, magnetic, photographic including photocopying, recording, or by any information storage and retrieval system without prior written permission of the publisher.

ISBNs:
Hardcover: 978-1-7372439-4-6

Paperback: 978-1-7372439-5-3

Ebook: 978—7372439-6-0

LOCC number: 2022918913

Writing, fiction, self-study

Book Design by ebookorprint.com

Lilac Publishing
271 Easy Street
Nancy, KY 42544

For: My parents, William and Donavee Vigus,

thanks for always believing in me.

FOREWORD

So, You Want to Write a Book?

As the award-winning author of the young adult fantasy series, I am often asked about the process of writing. How did you come up with the concept for your series? Where did you get your inspiration from? How did you create the fantasy world? How long did it take you to write the book?

While 81% of the world's population wish to write a book, most never do. In fact, most die with their book still in their head. Why? Certainly, it can't be THAT hard to write a book, right? Truth is many aspiring writers will be able to envision their book already completed, without them having put in any of the actual effort to write it. With Rebecka's book, however, you are in luck, because you are about to uncover the hidden secrets to writing.

I first met Rebecka at the 2017 Ann Arbor Book Festival our mutual publisher, at the time, had pre-arranged for us to participate in. It was my first scheduled author event, which I was very excited about, yet nervous. I didn't know anything about what it took to sell a book to a stranger. I didn't know who my book's target audience was or understood the multiple hats (roles) an author must wear to be successful. The one thing I did know was that I had somehow managed to write, finish and publish a book.

I found Rebecka to be wise, full of knowledge and someone I could learn from. We quickly became friends. Over the years, it has been my honor to watch her grow into *The Writer Whisperer*, where she coaches writers individually. She has demonstrated she knows no two writers are the same or at the same point in their writing journeys.

Rebecka's book is a treasure trove of information that is a must read for any aspiring writer and writers looking to improve their craft.

Rebecka will guide you through the process of getting your story written, revealing tools each aspiring writer should have at their disposal. You will take a deep dive into the various genres where Rebecka will share some of her own personal work as examples and encourage you to start creating your own story.

You will explore story types as well as learn what word counts are required to distinguish between a drabble, short story, novella, novel, etc. You will discover the different types of writers, the pantser, plantser and outliner, and explore which type of writer you are. You will examine your fears, discover what's holding you back, how to deal with the imposter syndrome and the dreaded writer's block. By the end of the book, you will have gained the knowledge necessary to get your book ready to send to an agent or a publisher!

If for whatever reason, should you decide to <u>not</u> complete the exercises found inside Rebecka's book, you will miss out on receiving the book's full value. Don't be one of the 81%!

I look forward to reading your book!

Mackenzie Flohr

<u>*The Rite of Wands*</u>

Introduction:

Am I Enough?

If you have chosen to purchase this book, you are interested in writing. Let me start off by telling you, writing is not a chore. It's not loneliness and missing out on life. Writing IS life! I do it because I am compelled to do it. Writing is a natural part of me. Everyone has a story to tell and anyone can be a writer. It is one of the most rewarding things I do.

At the age of ten, my teacher, Mr. Ireland, told me, with my imagination, one day he would see me in books. I believed him. I wrote nonsense poems for the next year and a half. Then, my family moved to a new town. I started junior high (seventh grade) in a school where friendships had been formed for years. I was the girl who didn't fit in. I wrote poems for the next six years on not fitting in. I also took every writing class I could take in high school. My teachers weren't the most helpful. I could get a paper back with a big red B on it and no comments, no obvious errors. How do you fix it? How do you know how to improve?

My parents let me submit a piece of writing to the Famous Writing School. A representative even came to the house. They laid out the program and the cost. If I were to take the program, there would be no college. What if I bombed? What if I couldn't get published? I chose to follow the path to college, where I majored in English, language, and literature. I also took every writing class I could fit into my schedule, journalism, feature writing, broadcast continuity writing, and narrative writing. I ruled out media writing as a career choice as it didn't allow for my imagination. I could hear Joe Friday whispering in my ear, "Just the facts, Ma'am."

In my narrative writing class, my instructor informed me, I had talent, but she didn't know how to develop it. Seriously? Why was I taking the class? Probably because I liked the instructor. Additionally, I was enjoying the class.

After college, I began writing poetry again. I entered dozens of poetry contests and did win an editor's choice award for one. I was included in eleven anthologies. Not what my heart wanted. I took the poems I had, typed them on an electric typewriter, had copies made at Kinkos, and took them to Reigle Press in Flint, Michigan, where they bound them into seventy-five books titled, *Only a Start.* One of the poems was introduced to the Michigan Senate as a possible state poem. The economy tanked, and for all I know, it is still in a pigeon-hole in some office building in Lansing, Michigan. Most of those books were given away.

Fast forward about ten years to when I found my first teaching job. I was going to teach special education and because I was forty credits into my master's degree in reading and learning disabilities. I was paid a beginning salary on a master's degree schedule. Big money, right? Wrong, it was about $19,222 for the year. I loved teaching, but still wanted to write. Colleagues encouraged me to redo my poetry book. I did and put some more current poetry with it. The book became, *Only a Start and Beyond.* I team taught with general education staff and since I was the writer, I taught the writing lessons. It was amazing!

In 2003, I was transferred to middle school to teach special education. At the end of the school year, one of my eighth-grade girls told me she couldn't wait to get to high school, meet a boy and have a baby. The resulting book, *So You Think You Want to be a Mommy?* debuted in 2004. While I now had two books under my belt, I still wanted to write a novel. Over spring break, I came up with an idea; however, after two false starts and a book going nowhere, I set it aside.

In November 2005, someone told me about National Novel Writing Month (NaNoWriMo). I looked it up on Google and signed up. I didn't start writing until November 8th. For those unfamiliar with this, the idea is to start at midnight on November 1st and write kamikaze style until midnight November 30th with the goal of writing a 50,000-word novel. I was sure I'd never reach 50,000 words, but I was going to give it a try. November 10th, I arrived home to no power. There would be no writing. I was about six hundred words in. I spent my weekend hammering on my keyboard to catch up. I had five chapters so, I printed it out and took it to school with me. During our reading class, I read it to my eighth-grade students and later to my seventh graders. I wanted feedback. I did fix a couple of glaring errors but no serious editing from then on, I had to give them a progress report on how many words I had written the night before and my total word count. Thus, twenty-one days after I started, *Secrets* was complete. Yes, I wrote 50,000 words and received my NaNoWriMo award certificate.

Now the fun began. I used the same publisher I had with the first two books. I did not realize they were a vanity press. I was making $0.89/book in royalties. This after I paid a substantial amount to be published in the first place. There was no marketing plan. I didn't even know how to market. Luckily, it sold about two hundred copies. I did not even break even.

The good thing was, I got requests for more books. I had credibility. It took me three more books to finally land a small press publisher. Then, three weeks before the second book in my series came out, they closed their doors. I became Lilac Publishing. While I was publishing my own books, I also took on four other authors. I had a great book designer and ran the company for six years. Until two things happened. First, Amazon announced they were closing Createspace, which is who did the printing for Lilac Publishing. Second, my book designer stopped designing book covers. He became my new publisher.

I still have one author whose books remain with Lilac Publishing. I am her only marketing outlet. I even went to Florida to do a joint book signing with her. Unfortunately, she was too ill to do the book signing, but her books were on display right next to mine. One of the other authors found a new publisher. One has stopped writing. The last one is busy reworking one of her books to make it longer for a new publisher.

If you are up to the challenge, I plan to guide you through the process of getting your story written and ready to send to an agent or publisher. You will get plenty to challenge your writing, your fears, your belief in yourself, and the actual writing of a novel. I have learned I AM enough. I believe YOU are enough.

See you inside,

Rebecka

Table of Contents

Part 1: Tools of the Trade 9
- Chapter 1: Gathering Your Tools 11
- Chapter 2: Learning to Use Your Tools 15
- Chapter 3: Facing Your Fears 21

Part 2: Taking the First Steps 25
- Chapter 4: Sampling the Genres 27
- Chapter 5: The Blank Piece of Paper 43
- Chapter 6: Building the Foundation 51

Part 3: Adding the Layers 53
- Chapter 7: Building Your Confidence 55
- Chapter 8: Following Your Blueprint 59
- Chapter 9: Finding Your Courage 67

Part 4: Finishing Touches 71
- Chapter 10: The Building is Complete 73
- Chapter 11: Who Are You? 77
- Chapter 12: Inspecting for Errors 81

Part 5: Up for Sale 85
- Chapter 13: Open House 87
- Chapter 14: Final Offer 89
- Chapter 15: Sold 95

Appendices 99
- Appendix A: Recommended Reading 101
- Appendix B: Writing Contests 105
- Appendix C: Job Application 107
- Acknowledgements 109
- About the Author 111

Part 1: Tools of the Trade

Chapter 1: Gathering Your Tools

In every field, there are tools. Artists, builders, teachers; even writers have tools. I'm going to give you a list of tools. Some will be familiar, others will not. I will share the reason for those not so obvious.

Here are the obvious ones: paper, pen, pencil, dictionary, thesaurus or synonym finder, a grammar book, a flash drive and/or external hard drive, computer and/or typewriter, and yourself.

The not so obvious ones: a journal, a small 3 x 5 notebook, multicolored flare pens, a calendar you can write in the squares, (these can be printed from a computer) a roll of adding machine or cash register tape, sticky notes, file folders, and a thick skin.

There are also some computer sites which may help you with your writing: Scrivener, Google Docs, Google sheets, Vellum, Freedom, Microsoft Word, Microsoft excel, Ulysses, ProWritingAid, and the Hemmingway App. Let me give you my understanding of each.

Scrivener is a program made for writers. It is a notebook view of your writing and can be broken into chapters or sections. It allows you to set a word count and keeps daily track. It will also allow you to set up for publishing with Barnes and Noble and Amazon. Cost for Mac is about $49 and for PC $45.

Google docs is free, easy to use, and everything is backed up in the cloud. It has collaborative capabilities and you can easily share it with your editor and later with beta readers.

Google sheets is a spreadsheet. *What on earth do you want a spreadsheet?* Several things. It's a great way to make an outline or event line. It makes a good character tracker. If you are writing a series, you don't want to keep referring to the first book to remember who your characters were. It's also free to share.

Vellum is a book formatting word processor. It will make your manuscripts into eBooks and paperbacks. It picks up where Scrivener, Google docs, and Microsoft word stop. Again, it is sharable. It runs $199 for eBooks and $249 for paperbacks. Unless you plan to self-publish, I would skip this one.

Freedom is a productivity app to help you stay on track. It allows your biggest distractions, scrolling online, messages, etc. from distracting you. Freedom lets you block these distractions for a set time-period. You can schedule different times throughout the day. When you hop on Facebook during a scheduled time, you will find it doesn't open. The cost for the pro version is $29/year.

Microsoft word is a word processor. The biggest drawback is the larger your work becomes, the harder it is to manage. Do not throw it out if it is all you have. Microsoft has varying prices depending on which program you use. I have thirteen published books all done on Microsoft word. It can be sharable.

Microsoft excel is a spreadsheet and will do much of what Google sheets do. Look into Microsoft programs to find which is best for you.

Ulysses is a word processor like Scrivener; however, it was not made for writers and you need to work with it to get it set up in a way you can use. It is made for Mac and allows you to sync all your work so you can work from different locations. The cost is about $45.

ProWritingAid is a grammatical/spell check program. If you struggle with grammar and sentence structure, this program goes beyond spell check. It has two versions and a pro version: one is free and the pro version costs $60. I have the free version. I find it frustrating after making changes it does not recognize them and still tells me they are wrong. It is also difficult to remove their edits from your manuscript. I had a client who used Grammarly and it took days to get their edits out.

Hemmingway App is a grammatical/spell checker. While similar to ProWritingAid and Grammarly, the paid app is cheaper coming in at $19.99. Grammarly is the most well-known but, costs double what ProWritingAid charges.

I use predominantly Microsoft ord. I have used Google docs when I know it is something I will have to share. You need to explore the options and find out what works well for you and your budget.

Which seems most daunting? For some, it's just a collection of the obvious ones. Do gather them as well as the not so obvious ones and put them in your writing space.

Oh, wait, writing space? Yes, you need a writing space. It doesn't have to be a full-blown office. Just a space you create for your writing. If you don't have one, now is the time to create one.

If you have an unused corner in a room, put a small writing table there and a place to keep your supplies. I am fortunate in being able to have an office. The third bedroom in my house has no closet. It originally was home to a pair of peacocks. I turned it into an office with a daybed just in case someone needs to sleep there. I have two bookshelves, my desk, and a two-drawer file cabinet. I keep a cup warmer so, I have a place for my tea. I also have a spot for my water bottle. Since I work on a laptop, I can transport my work to any room in the house. My office offers me a view of my front yard and the driveway, so I know if someone is approaching. It also lets me enjoy the nature surrounding my home. You create a space you can work in. Music is allowed, but not the television.

I'm also giving you a list of words to lose from your writing. Keep these handy and refer to them.

Words to lose:

could, should, would, have, has, had, been, is, are, was, were, that, and ,and.

Yes, there is a comma in front of and, I put it there for a reason.

In your journal: I want you to start doing Morning Pages. They were created by Julia Cameron. Set aside 90 minutes every morning, even if it means you get up earlier. Write three (3) hand-written pages. Anything on your mind. Your anxieties, an issue at work, with your significant other, kids, bills, money in general, a co-worker, the weather, anything. Whatever is in your mind goes on the paper. Every single morning. These pages are brain dumps, you get everything bothering you out and then are free to go about your day. The pages are yours and yours alone. If you make a spelling error, cross it out and keep going. No one is checking grammar, run-on sentences, fragments, or anything else. This is to get you writing.

The other task you have is to gather all your tools, put them in your writing space, take a photo of it, post it in the FB group, and report back when you are ready for the next session.

Chapter 2: Learning to Use Your Tools

I'm not going to explain the obvious tools. You have been using the for years. I'm sure you are an expert with them.

Let's start with a journal. It is often the least used and most helpful item on the list. It's a place to keep your ideas, dreams, and goals. It's a place to keep your characters and some of their traits. Do you know how frustrating it is to have to scroll back in your work because you can't remember something about your character or a secondary character's name? Keep it handy. Do a journal for each work-in-progress (WIP). Keep it separate from your Morning Pages.

A small 3 x 5 notebook is the next one. It can flip open or side open. You can find them in packs of three or five at the dollar store. Put one in your purse or pocket to carry with you all the time. You never know when something might spark an idea and you need to write it down before you forget. I keep one next to my bed. I have been known to wake up with an idea and need to write it down. If I don't, it will be lost by the time I wake up in the morning.

Multicolored flare pens are what I use for editing. I use a different color each time I edit. This prevents me from making the same edit twice and it helps me see where they are when I go to put them into my computer.

A calendar which you can write in the squares. I generally use a large desk calendar. This is where your pencil will come in handy. You are going to be charting your progress. First, put a start date on your calendar. The goal is to write a 50,000-word novel. Yes, you can write more. We are using 50,000 words as a starting point. Assume most pages will take 250 words. On the days you write, you need to write at least 250 words. If you are only writing on Saturday and

Sunday, you might want to write more. If you choose to write only weekends, you have 104 days of writing at 250 words giving you 26,000 words. By writing 500 words a day, you will come out with 52,000 words.

Some days you will be on a roll and may not want to stop writing; this is a good thing. There will be days when you can write 1,000 words and days where 100 words will feel like torture. It happens. It's okay to walk away.

If you are writing five days a week at 250 words, you have 1,250 words each week. By week fifty-two, you should have 65,000 words. This makes 50,000 words doable.

On your calendar, pencil in 250 words a day for the days you are writing. As you start writing, put your actual word count on the calendar at the end of your writing time. Tally the actual words at the end of the week. Treat yourself if you met or exceeded your goal.

The cash register or adding machine tape is needed to make your event line. The event line reflects the things happening in your story

    What is the starting event?

    What is the reaction to the event?

    Does it create a roadblock for your main character?

    How is the roadblock overcome?

    Does overcoming the roadblock lead the next event?

What changes does your main character go through?

When we talk about characters and motivation this will become clearer.

I find I am forever jotting something on a sticky note and taping it to the corner of my computer or in a file I'm keeping for my WIP. I use them to keep track of release dates, launch parties, book events, book signings, speaking events, etc. They are just handy to have. I have also used pinup.com to keep track of things. You can also use note.ly. Again, find what works for you.

Physical file folders have several uses. I try to keep one for my WIP; however, I sometimes have two or three WIPs going on at once. A while back I printed each chapter when I finished it and placed it in a file folder. It was a way to keep me from going back to do edits.

A thick skin is needed when you send your book to an editor, and when rejections or reviews start coming in. Your editor may think you left out some important details or need to omit an entire chapter. Remember their goal is to make your book the best it can be.

Reviewers might not like your book. Not everyone will. Don't take it personally. It might be it's not the genre they normally read. They may disagree with your premise. It might just have been a bad day. You will never know. The important thing is to see if there is anything you can learn from a review. **Never** under any circumstances reply to a review good or bad. Let your work stand on its own merits. Your readers have not walked in your shoes and might just have a different opinion. It's all good.

Now for **the words to lose**. Many of these are verbs, I'm aware of it. They are past tense verbs. Past tense is passive voice. You want active voice in your writing. You generally want present tense unless it is a memory or flashback. We have now taken care of the first eleven words.

We come to "that" a word so over-used and used incorrectly it makes me crazy. I am not a Grammar Nazi. This, however, is my biggest pet peeve with writers. When using the word "that" it **must** refer to a specific person, place, thing, or idea. For example: that house, that book, that girl, that brilliant idea. If you are not using it to identify something specific, don't use it. Replace it with who, which, it, or omit it completely. Once you have finished writing your book, in your word program under editing, select **find** and type in 'that." Note how many times you used the word. Then read each sentence and ask yourself is there a better word. Rewrite the sentence if necessary.

For the first twelve words on the list, know you will use them sometimes. Not using them will make your writing more concise. There won't be anything vague in your writing. I still search for them in each book I write. I even go back and change the sentence or omit the words.

Now for, ",and" this is my second pet peeve. You use a comma before the word and, if you are listing things. You use a comma before and, if you are connecting two sentences which are related but could stand alone.

Incorrect use: He picked up the stone, and skipped it across the lake.

Correct use: He picked up the stone and skipped it across the lake.

Correct use: I gave you a list of obvious tools, not so obvious tools, and words to lose.

Correct use: Tommy ran all the way home, and the boys chasing him were unable to catch him before he reached the front door.

In this sentence I could have written: Tommy ran all the way home. The boys chasing him were unable to catch him before he reached the front door.

Both examples are correct. The second example is a bit wordy, If I took more time, I probably could have come up with a better sentence.

Here's your **assignment.** Look at a novel you are currently reading. The page you are on is your focus. How many words are over-used? Remember you will use them occasionally. How many times do you find the word "that" on the page? How many times do you find it more than once in the same sentence?

Pick one paragraph, find the **over-used** words. Write it as it is in the book. Then write it better. Put the name of the book and the author. We are not author bashing. We are looking at how many authors do this. We are also not critiquing other writers in this class. We are looking to see the **over-used** words, "that," or ",and." There is a file in the Facebook page for this class. Put your assignment there. Make a comment, **at least let someone** know you read their assignment.

_____
_____
_____
_____
_____
_____
_____
_____
_____
_____
_____
_____
_____
_____

Chapter 3: Facing Your Fears

Before you can do any writing, you must face your fears.

1. What is keeping you from writing?

2. Why haven't you begun the novel you want to write?

3. Are you afraid of failing?

4. Are you afraid you won't be taken seriously?

5. Are you stuck in a rut?

6. Are you telling yourself, you don't have time?

7. Is it something else?

All those fears can be overcome. The question I'm asking is *do you want to write a novel?* If the answer is yes, we will work on your fears. If the answer is no, stop here.

Yes, the last sentence seemed harsh. It is, however, the truth. If you don't want to write a novel, this will be a waste of your time. I am not here to waste time. I'm here to help those who want to write a novel get it done. So, let's look at these fears.

Time is a huge factor in writing. You *must* make time to write. You should be writing *every day*, even if it's only Morning Pages to start. I used to tell people to mark out writing time on their calendars. I'm going to tell you to write when you have time, during your morning coffee break, at lunch, if you commute by transit; write during your commute. Write after the kids have gone to bed. Just as long as you are writing. Don't skip date night with your significant other to write.

You may choose to write only five days a week and leave your weekends to spend with family and friends. Super, fantastic! You may be the person who only wants to write on

Saturday and Sunday, and you are planning to block out time to do this. Go for it! You are in charge of when you write.

You are also in charge of where you write, at the kitchen table, a small office, in a park, library, a special spot in the backyard, your favorite coffee shop, even a cemetery. Pick your spot. You might even dictate your story for later transcription. As Michael Jordan would say, "Just do it!" Now we have taken care of the time issue, find what works for you.

Are your friends and family telling you writing will never make you any money? Do they suggest you should quit before you start? Turn off the naysayers. They are jealous because you are following your dream. Follow the dream. My classmates laughed at me all through high school because I wanted to be a writer. Others just rolled their eyes. Guess who some of my biggest fans are? Those same people who laughed or rolled their eyes.

Are you feeling like I did? What if my writing isn't good enough? You will never know the answer if you do not try. Set aside those fears and write. I'll be here to guide you. I believe in you. I know in my heart YOU can do this. From this point on, we are going to embrace your fears, worries, doubts, excuses, and procrastination. We will make them your positives.

Your Assignment: Make a writing contract with yourself. Include 90 minutes in the morning for Morning Pages. Include your desire to write when you have time, then make the time. Include once a week solo Artist Dates* to the library, park, museum, artist gallery, craft store, the coffee shop, the mall to people watch, a hike in the woods, fishing in a stream or lake, be a tourist in your own town or state, wine and painting, paint ceramics, make pottery, the possibilities are endless. Sign and date your contract and post it in the file on the Facebook page. Look at what the others have posted. Give them a thumbs up. You can also post pictures of your Artist Dates, maybe they will inspire others.

*Artist Dates are also the creation of Julia Cameron. Their use is to allow your senses to absorb the sights, sounds, smells, tastes of your surroundings and to recharge your creative self.

_____

_____

_____

_____

_____

_____

_____

_____

_____

_____

_____

_____

_____

_____

_____

_____   _____
              Sign   Date

Part 2: Taking the First Steps

Chapter 4: Sampling the Genres

Before you can write anything, you need to know the genre you plan to write in. You need to know for three reasons.

1) There are rules for each one.

2) You need to know the category you are writing in for marketing purposes.

3) You need to know the audience you are writing for.

We are going to discuss most of the fiction genres in this lesson. Genre, according to dictionary.com, *is a class or category of an artistic endeavor having particular form, content, or technique.*

The following are the genres we will be looking at:

Flash fiction

Fan fiction

Mystery/crime

Cozy mystery

Science Fiction (Sci-fi)

Young Adult (YA)

Beginning Chapter books (grades 3-5)

Children's books (picture, alphabet)

Middle grades (4-8)

Fairytales

Horror/paranormal/ghost

Romance

Historical Romance

Fantasy

Chick lit

Steampunk

Military

Psychological thriller

Thriller/suspense

Humorous fiction

LGBTQ+

These are the most common genres of fiction. I'm sure if you looked, you could find others as well as subcategories of each. These are the ones we will deal with.

Flash fiction has a specific word count. It can be anywhere from 300 to 1500 words and is generally no longer than 1500 words. This is where you all gasp. I know I did when I first heard about it. My question was, how do you fit an entire story into 1500 words, forget considering 300 words. It can be done and has been done well. I have even written flash fiction. My first was 997 words about a fairy named Twitter, Twit for short. She was a smashing hit.

Let's start with flash fiction. I'm going to share with you a piece I wrote. Remember, I am a novelist and never dreamed flash fiction could possibly be something I would write.

The Vault

The gym was filled with people. The voices mingled in Megan's head. She'd warmed up and would soon be ready to vault, her best event. The team was counting on her.

She stepped to the side of the track and waited for the judges to wave their flag. When they did, she saluted and stepped onto the track. She heard the shouts, "Go, Tiny!" Above them was her father's voice yelling, "Go, Megan!" She began her run toward the vault. Her focus was on hitting the springboard correctly. Hands out, no bent elbows, feet together, toes pointed, over the vault, and stick the landing.

She did it. With a big smile, she turned and presented to the judges. Her coach hugged her, gave her some last-minute guidance and sent her back to do it again. She wanted to wave to her family but it was not allowed during competition. She had to get her mind focused on the next vault. She knew the best one was the only one scored.

Again, she waited for the signal from the judges. She could see her family, Mom, Dad, Jason, and Granny. Already her parents and those of her teammates were shouting, "Go, Tiny!" She ran as fast as she could counting her steps to hit the springboard in the right place. Hands out, no bent elbows, feet together, toes pointed, over the vault, and stick the landing. She knew the landing was perfect.

With her big smile, she presented to the judges. She got a hug from her coach and a pat on the back. This time she waved to the family. Everyone cheered when the score came up; 9.575.

The last vault she would make as a competitive gymnast.

For those of you counting this was 288 words and considered a drabble. As a postscript, Megan did compete again. She did high school gymnastics for four years but, has never gone back to club gymnastics. A foot injury will keep her from competing in the sport again. She is lucky enough to coach part-time with her mom who is the Varsity Head Coach at her old high school.

Some pieces of flash fiction are personal narratives.

Assignment: Take a single incident from your life and write it as a piece of flash fiction (not more than 1500 words less is better). **Post it in the Facebook group in the files. Read the ones posted and leave some positive feedback.**

_____

_____

_____

_____

_____

_____

_____

_____

_____

_____

Fan fiction is fiction written based on someone else's writing. Godzilla has thousands of fans who have written fan fiction pieces about Godzilla. They submit them to fan sites. I personally have an author friend who is a huge Dr. Who fan. Her book series is widely acclaimed. It is in fact about a young wizard. The Walking Dead has fan fiction writers as does the Game of Thrones. I know a writer who wrote a book using the premise of the Game of Thrones secret society. It was a good first book and I wish she would write the second. For most people writing fan fiction is not a money maker, it's more of a contest to see who can write the best. Every fan believes they can write the best fan fiction. Fan fiction is only publishable on the fan website.

Mystery/crime is fiction based on solving a crime. This leaves writers free to write about any crime they can imagine. There are some good characters in this genre. James Patterson's Alex Cross is a Washington DC police officer who specializes in criminal psychology. Michael

Connelly's Harry Bosch is an LAPD homicide investigator. Patricia Cornwell's Kay Scarpetta is a medical examiner. Sara Paretsky's V.I. Warshawski is a private investigator. William Kent Krueger's Corcoran O'Connor is half-Irish, half-Anishinabe Indian sheriff. If you are not familiar with any of these authors or characters, please read at least one book by each author. Some mysteries dwell on the investigation, some on the courtroom, some on autopsy. Others deal with why did the incident happen? What makes a person do what they do? Motive.

Cozy mysteries are solved by little old ladies think *Murder She Wrote*. You don't see the gruesome side of murders. Agatha Christy was the queen of cozy mysteries. Remember these are usually sweet little ladies who would abhor the ugly side of crime. The Mrs. Pollifax mysteries by Dorothy Gillman is a good example of a cozy mystery series. Debbie Macomber's Cedar Cove Series would fall into the cozy category.

Science fiction or Sci-fi is exactly what it implies the study of science in a fictional way. Experiments which could not happen in real science being invisible is one. At one time, putting a man on the moon was considered science fiction. Ray Bradbury is probably the king of science fiction writing. You need to know something about science before attempting this genre.

Young adult (YA) is written for high school or college age readers. It is everyday life with a twist. The Twilight books are YA so, are the Harry Potter books. The Hunger Games are YA albeit badly written. I say this because I was less than ten pages in the first book and knew how the book would end. I also know when Susan Collins tried to sell them at huge book expo in Las Vegas, she couldn't even give them away. Had someone in Hollywood not seen a way to use special effects to bring the story to life, it would have died.

Beginning chapter books (grades 3-5 or ages 8-10): These books are meant to teach something. They are written simply to engage the reader while giving a life lesson. This is where books like Cam Jansen come in. Cam has a photographic memory. When she wants to remember something, she looks at it and says, "Click." Later she will use the stored memory to help her solve whatever issue is at hand. Nate the Great books, also fall into this category. He has great adventures. They are not more than 60 pages long.

Children's picture/alphabet books are just what they say they are. They are books of pictures. The first type of book children will be exposed to. They include nursery rhymes, Dr. Seuss books, and alphabet books. Maurice Sendak is wonderful with picture books. He illustrates his own. Just think of all the wonderful creatures in *Where the Wild Things Are.* Sometimes these are harder to write than a full-length novel. You need a good illustrator as the illustrations help tell the story. The story must have a meaning children will grasp or in the case of Dr. Seuss, they are rhyming books.

Middle grade books (grades 4-8 ages 10-15): They are high adventure books. While they can be high adventure, there is usually a lesson in them. They are about children usually a group of kids working together to accomplish something. The following is an example of a middle grade flash fiction piece I wrote for a Halloween anthology.

Finding Ghosts

Teddy Brinker and Tommy Huff were the best of friends. They were also as different as night and day. Teddy was stocky with huge brown eyes and chocolate brown hair. Tommy the other hand was slender and blond with sky blue eyes. At twelve, they felt too old for traditional trick or treating. This year they planned to capture a ghost. They had a five dollar bet going as to whether or not ghosts really existed.

For weeks they had planned how they were going to do this. The decision was to camp in a tent in Teddy's backyard and sneak to the cemetery after all the trick or treaters were inside. Since Tommy had to take his younger brother and sister out to collect candy, the boys were going in camouflage with their faces blackened. They had been stocking up on flashlights and batteries both had cameras and by Friday night they'd be stocked up on munchies. The plan was perfect.

It rained all day Thursday the boys were bummed, as they really wanted to be able to sleep out. The tent was to go up after school tomorrow.

"Rain finally quit," Teddy said as they walked home from school.

Tommy shrugged, "I guess."

"We'll see ghosts, I know we will," Teddy assured him.

"No such thing as ghosts," Tommy retorted.

"Betcha five dollars we see some."

"You're on."

The boys raced each other home. The plan was to put all the supplies together tonight so they wouldn't waste time with them tomorrow.

Friday dawned with the sun shining brightly. The boys could hardly wait for school to get out so they could get into the good stuff. Heading for Teddy's after school they talked about the night.

"First, we have to take my brother and sister out," Tommy was saying. "So, we might as well put on our camouflage and pretend we are still young enough to enjoy it. Then, my mom will have food for us when we get back. After we eat, we'll go to your house, check in, and see to the tent."

"That's the plan," Teddy agreed. "Once my folks do a final check on us and turn out the lights, we'll head for the cemetery. I'm glad we scoped it out ahead of time and found a way in by the creek."

"Yeah, me, too."

"This is going to be so much fun."

At Teddy's they set up the tent and put all their supplies inside. Then, they took out their camouflage and painted each other's faces. Mrs. Brinker took their picture. The boys were impatient and took off for Tommy's as soon as she was done.

Tommy's brother and sister were waiting for them. "Hurry up, Tommy! We're going to miss the good stuff," his brother yelled.

They trudged from house to house in their neighborhood hollering, "Trick or Treat!" at each door they came to. Tommy found himself having more fun that he thought he would. Teddy didn't say much but he was collecting candy with the rest of them.

When they were done, they headed to the park for donuts and cider. There they were able to get candy from the shopkeepers in town. After they finished, they went back to Tommy's house for a dinner of barbeque beef sandwiches and what his mom called, "Witches' Brew," hot Dr. Pepper. They cleaned their plates and put them in the dishwasher, grabbed their loot and headed for Teddy's.

At Teddy's, Tommy made his call home to let his mom know he was there safely. Then the boys took their candy and headed to the tent. They set up the battery lantern, rolled out the sleeping bags, and dumped out their goodies. After swapping for the ones they liked best, they ate some of the chips and jerky Teddy had provided. They also had a cooler of pop Teddy managed to sneak from the house.

Mr. Brinker came out about ten to check on them. "I'll leave the back door unlocked in case you decide to come inside."

"Thanks, Dad," Teddy said. Then they heard the back door shut. "Turn out the lights and we'll watch for them to go to sleep."

With the lights out the boys laid on their sleeping bags watching the Brinkers turn out the lights and head to bed. When the last light went out, Teddy said, "Thirty minutes and we're good to go."

Tommy loaded his pockets with candy, grabbed his flashlight, and camera. He was ready when Teddy whispered, "Now."

They slipped into the darkness, out of the yard, and followed the path to the back of the cemetery. Earlier in the week they had scoped out the best way in. Once inside, they stealthily moved to the biggest stone they could find. The plan was falling into place. One boy seated on either side of the tombstone. They put their cameras in their laps and settled in to wait. Both had pop and candy.

Tommy jumped when he heard Teddy pop the top of his drink can. It sounded loud in the darkness. "Did you hear that?"

"It's my pop," Teddy sounded exasperated. He knew Tommy didn't believe in ghosts and hadn't wanted to come.

They settled in again. The next sound either of them heard was candy wrappers. Finally, they settled down and only the sounds of the night were heard the hooting of an owl, the wings of bats, and the song of night birds. Fog rose from the river and surrounded the cemetery. Tommy was sure all they were going to get out of this was pneumonia. He was cold and damp just sitting there.

Teddy screamed. Tommy shot up with his camera ready. He started clicking the button. The flash went off and a huge white form floated away. "Did you get it?" Teddy wanted to know.

"I'll check," Tommy answered, checking the photo on his digital camera. "All I can see is a white sheet with dark eye holes."

"Let me see," Teddy said reaching for the camera. He glanced down. It looked fake. "It's jus a sheet." He gave Tommy back the camera and sat back down. Tommy sat on his side of the tombstone and studied the picture on his camera.

Something flew above his head close enough to create a breeze, Tommy looked up. He grabbed his camera and took another picture.

"What are you doing?" Teddy asked, standing to yell at his friend. He was stunned as something floated above Tommy's head. Tommy continued taking pictures. The vision appeared to be hovering. Teddy reached for it and his hand went right through it. "Run, Tommy!" he shouted as he grabbed his stuff and started running.

He stopped at the fence to see if Tommy was behind him. He saw the flash from the camera. Then it stopped. Tommy slowly made his way to Teddy.

"Let's see what I got," he said.

They made their way quickly back to the tent where they sat down to look at the photos Tommy had taken. "It's not a ghost," Tommy said in awe, "It was an angel watching over us. There are no ghosts pay up."

Teddy gave Tommy five dollars they had bet and leaned back on his sleeping bag to think about what just happened.

Mr. Brinker found them still dressed and sound asleep the next morning. He smiled. The hologram had worked; his ghost hunters thought they'd seen a ghost. Things could go back to normal. He went to call Mr. Huff.

In memory of John Brinkerhuff

Fairytales are magical. They capture a life different from our own. They are loved by all ages. You can create fairytales. You do not have to find a new take on the old ones. I have a 64-page book of fairytales titled, *Of Moonbeams and Fairies: Collected Tales.* It has been my best seller by far. I have found adults like it as much as children do. I have had requests for more tales of Twitter the Fairy.

Horror/paranormal/ghosts fit into this category. They are books written about horrific things, paranormal experiences, or ghosts among us. For this genre you need to this think Stephen King. He has horror down to a science. I believe he can write it in his sleep. These are hot selling books right now. Werewolves, vampires, and the like are in demand.

Romance is about love and relationships. At one time, it was scripted. Emily Loring wrote romance. In every one of her novels there was an heiress, two men were courting her, and of course, a roadster. Her books worked because you never knew which of the two men she would choose and sometimes it was the wrong guy right up to the end.

They can be set in any era. If you choose to write historical romance, please know the era you are writing about. Your readers will know and will let you know if you get it wrong. In the book, *Elizabeth,* by Tasha Alexander was written as a companion to the movie, she noted in the front of the book there were things in the book not in historical order. She is a writer of historical fiction and goes out of her way to make sure her facts are correct, even though her characters are fictional.

Which leads us to **historical fiction/romance**. This is fiction written about an historical event, person, or era. There have been many stories written about the Revolutionary War and the Civil War. They have been written about kings and queens in foreign nations, about nations during different eras. There are fiction books written about the Battle of the Little Big Horn. It is *critical* to do the research if you want to be believable. You want your readers to know you are credible. If you cast King Arthur as a Roman soldier who came to the crown of England with his wife, Carlotta, who was a Moor and not Guinevere, you will take heat in your reviews. This is not what you want. Accuracy is important in historical fiction and romance.

Fantasy or other realms is a wide-open field. David Baldacci, who writes compelling mysteries, also wrote a YA fantasy series, which is being made into a series of movies. It is a four-book series starting with *The Finisher*. He introduces us to Vega Jane, who questions everything in a community where no one is supposed questions anything. Her big questions are: What is on the other side of the Quag? What happened to her parents?

You can create a world for your characters. You can create the creatures who inhabit this world. This is where dragons come to life. Think *The Neverending Story*, which is the epic adventure story. Fairies and elves can be a part of this world. Trees can talk. Magic can be a central part but, in the end, something really big is going to take place.

Chick lit is generally written by women for women about things women are interested in. There can be romance or failed romance. There could be some suspense, but the goal is to write about things women will find amusing, entertaining, or they know someone who could be the main character. These are lighthearted books.

Steampunk combines technology with the Victorian Era (late 19th century) and science fiction. It's interesting. There is an entire steampunk fan group. They dress as if they are in Victorian Era in costumes with cogs and other gadgetry attached to their clothing or woven into the cloth itself. You need to be extremely familiar with technology, science fiction, and the Victorian Era. This would be where Sherlock Holmes meets the iPhone.

Military fiction is written about special operatives, battles, missions, and different wars. It is big picture writing. There is a threat to the known world. To write this you must know about the military, politics, special ops groups, where they might be deployed, and what objectives they might have. This would include, but not be limited to mercenary soldiers, para-military groups, covert operations, even rebels in a third world country.

Finally, there are **psychological thrillers.** This type of fiction explores the mind of the main character who commits atrocities before being caught. What makes the person the psychopath he/she has become? This is one about serial killers who have been caught or police are trying to catch. They are people who have an everyday life but, also a secret life where they commit heinous crimes. Knowing something about behavioral psychology is a big help when writing this type of story. Digging into the mind of another person must be done without becoming the character you write about.

Thriller/suspense: These tend to be mysteries, on a large scale. There is a threat, plot, potential event which could destroy a state, country, or the world. There could be an uprising.

It could be political, there could be atrocities. Some of them are horror of epic proportions. These books will make you sit on the edge of your seat. You will not want to stop turning pages. These are the books; you are still reading at 3am. John Gilstrap writes these extremely well.

Humorous fiction is exactly what is says it is. It is humor. It can be in any or all of the above genres. Janet Evanovich writes it in her mystery series starting with *One for the Money*. The point is to tell a story allowing you to laugh.

LGBTQ+ has not officially been named a genre. Partly because it fits into any of the genres. Before you attempt to write this type of fiction, please go the following blog and read what this author says about the subject. https://www.how-to-write-a-book-now.com/about-lgbt-as-a-genre.html * I don't ever want to see stereotypes if you are writing this genre.

These are the genres of fiction.

*I was given permission by the author of the blog to use it here.

Your assignment: First, take a deep breath and think about the kind of fiction you want to write. I started with mysteries because, I like putting a puzzle together and following clues to put the bad guy in prison. Mysteries are puzzles needing to be solved. Then, figure out what genre you are writing. Make sure you are reading books in your genre. You are not looking for ideas, you are reading to know what is already out there. Put down your chosen genre and at least 4 books you have read in that genre. Include the title and author of the book. Post in the FB group

Genre _____

1. _____

2. _____

3. _____

4.

Chapter 5: The Blank Piece of Paper

If you are anything like me, when the English teacher said, "Clean off your desk and take out a blank sheet of paper." I cringed. She would begin writing four or five topics on the chalkboard. Inevitably, I would have no interest in any of the topics she had written. My mind was suddenly blank. It's like, if she put a gun to my head, I couldn't have written my own name, much less some essay.

Well, today you are taking out a blank sheet of paper. Unlike the English teacher, I am not giving you topics to write on. I'm going to help you generate ideas for writing.

On your paper write, **People I Know**, then number 1-3. Write the names of three people you know well and could write about. Please do not write celebrity names unless you have had dinner at their homes on a regular basis. I want the names of people you know well. My list is as follows:

1) Jamie
2) Gran
3) Dean

Your list:

1._____

2._____

3._____

Next on your paper write, **Places I've Been** and number from 1-3. Write three places you have been to preferably more than once. My list is as follows:

1) Las Vegas

2) Kiawah Island, SC

3) Gaylord, MI

Your list:

1._____

2._____

3._____

Continuing on your paper write, **Things I Like to Do**, and number 1-3. Write the top three things you like to do. My list is as follows:

1) Swim

2) Crochet

3) Read

Your list:

1._____

2._____

3._____

The next list on your paper write, **Things I Love to Eat**, and number 1-3. Write the top three things you like to eat. My list is as follows:

1) Chocolate

2) Shrimp or chicken fajitas

3) Hot fudge sundaes

Your list:

1._____

2._____

3._____

Now look at your lists.

1) Who can you write about?

2) What setting can you put them in?

3) Are they doing something they like?

4) Is eating involved?

The following is my personal narrative. This happened in real life.

This is the Way, I Remember It

It was a warm and sunny August morning the smell of bacon and eggs mingled with the smell of campfires. Kids in the campground used waxed paper bread wrappers to wax the slide in the playground. My Aunt Rosie showed up with my younger brother, Dean, who wanted to go up the slide. I followed him up the ten-foot slide. When he got to the top, he looked down and was frightened. Rosie told me to give him a push and she'd catch him at the bottom.

So, I gave him a big shove. Dean stiffened as he flew down the slippery slide. Rosie could not get to the bottom fast enough. Dean screamed on impact. My mom heard him at our campsite, grabbed my baby sister, and came running. Dad finished shutting everything up and followed in the car.

We loaded into the car. Dean was lying across my parents' laps. His head was on Mom and his legs were on Dad. I was frightened. I wasn't sure what had happened, only my brother had been hurt and I had pushed him.

At the hospital, they splinted my brother's legs together. One was broken in two places. We had a choice to take him to Traverse City or to Hurley Medical Center in Flint. We lived in Flint, so it was decided to go home. We had rented the campsite for two weeks. My dad stopped in at the rangers' station to tell them what had happened, and he'd be back on the weekend to get everything.

It was the longest ride home ever. Dean cried every time we hit a bump on the road. Once Dad got Mom and Dean into the emergency room, he took the rest of us home. Rosie took the blame for everything, but I knew it was my fault Dean's leg was broken.

I got physically sick with the guilt of hurting him. Mom and Dad were confused because I didn't have a fever and seemed fine during the day but would be up all night heaving my guts out. It took three days for them to finally get me to tell them it was my fault Dean was hurt. I was the one who pushed him.

Once I told them, we talked about how it really was no one's fault it was an accident. I started feeling better. It took some time for me to realize and come to terms with the fact things could have been done differently which might have prevented the accident to begin with. While there was no lasting damage from the broken leg, it will always be something I remember.

I was five and a half years old when this incident took place. My brother was two and a half at the time. He grew to be a healthy six feet tall.

Personal narratives are usually isolated incidents which have an impact on our lives.

*Your assignment will be to look at your list. Write about an incident in your life which made a significant impact on your life. In a narrative there is rarely any talking. It is the author remembering and telling the story. You need only write 1-2 pages. Narratives are not long. Some people use narratives to tell their own story. Each chapter in their memoir tells a story about their lives until they have finished writing the book. Post yours to the Facebook group. Read each other's and post some positive comments. We are not looking for criticism here.

———————————————

Chapter 6: Building the Foundation

Every good story or book has a good foundation. We are going to start in this chapter building the foundation for your story.

Whether you are starting with an idea, a premise, or a character, we are going to start. The idea/premise is the idea of what will happen. A bank robbery, a terror attack, a missing person, a new love, or high fantasy. Whatever idea you have is where you will start.

On the other hand, if you have an idea for a character and can describe this person, this is where you will start.

In all cases, you will start with an event line. This is where your adding machine/cash register tape will come into play. You are going to use this line to introduce your main character and put him/her into action.

*In case you are not sure, here is an exercise to get you started. **Choose one** from the following and create a scene from it.

1) It's raining, you see a person stumbling out of a dark alley and heading to a light on the side of a diner.

2) There is a fire at a downtown warehouse. The building is empty, but when the fire is out, they find a body.

3) An amber alert comes across your phone: a young girl is missing. She went to school but did not return home at the end of the day. The worried parents called the police and a search is underway.

4) On her long-awaited vacation to a tropical island, your character runs into someone not seen in years. They meet for dinner and sparks fly.

5) The chemistry lab at school has been broken into. Several items are missing. Police are investigating whether it was kids or something more serious.

6) The twins are identical, even their parents have trouble telling them apart. They often sit in on the other's classes. What kind of havoc does this create?

7) It had been raining for six weeks straight. People were tired of the rain and some areas were flooding. The local dam is about to break.

8) Your character is an investigative reporter. What is being investigated? How much danger is involved?

9) A local band has made the big time. One of the members gets involved with drugs while the band is on tour. What kind of fallout comes from this?

10) The boys found an abandoned fort in the woods. When they go to explore it the next time, they find someone had been living there.

Now look at your own story.

1) How will you introduce your main character?

2) How will you grab your reader and pull them in?

3) What is the setting and how will you describe it?

This does not need to be posted yet. We are doing layering in the next chapter.

If you don't have an idea for your story and want to use one of the above story starts, please feel free to do so. I could give you all the same start and each of you would produce a different story. Some might parallel, but no two would be the same.

Part 3: Adding the Layers

Chapter 7: Building Your Confidence

You should have a beginning to your story. The questions are:

1) Are you confident someone will want to read it?

2) Do you know your character?

3) Are you comfortable with the setting?

4) Have you initiated the action?

Let's start with your character.

1)Have you filled out a job application for him/her? You will find one in Appendix C. You may make as many copies as you need for your characters.

If you don't want to fill out a job application, fill out the following:

Name: First, middle, last. If there is a designation, use it: i.e.: Jr. Sr. II, III, Ph.D., etc. Yes, your character **must** have a first and last name. Exceptions are allowed for fairies, elves, fictional creatures, aliens, etc.

Age: Give them a birth date, April 18, 1994, is an example and their given age. In this case, the age is twenty-nine.

Male/female/transgender is important for you to know. It may or may not be a pivotal part of the story, but you should know.

Race: While it seems odd for me to say this, it's not. I was reading a friend's book and halfway through she mentioned the girls were black. Really? At this point it made no difference. It did change how I envisioned them. Don't hide the character's race. Even if the story has nothing to do with race, don't hide it. Don't spring it on your reader halfway through the book.

Physical description is never left to your reader's imagination. Hair color, eye color, height, build, weight (not always necessary unless you are Jack Reacher, who is six feet four inches, 238 pounds and has fists like hammers. Oh, and he's already been done).

How does your character speak? Midwestern, southern with a slight drawl or heavy drawl, northeastern, (Bohston area). You need to know any nuances in their speech. Do they have a pet phrase? Don't use it unless the phrase is called for.

Where do they work? What is their title and position?

What is their education? Are they streetwise? Did they attend college or the school of hard knocks?

Do they have recognizable attire? A watch, piece of jewelry, always wears and ascot, tends to wear shades of grey, things of this nature.

What are they like? What kind of personality to they have? Do others like them? Or talk about them behind their backs? Are they kind? Do they think they are above others (servants, doormen, anyone they feel does a menial job)? Do they have pets? Do they like children?

What do they do in their down time? Are they athletes? Sports buffs? Do they attend the theater, art galleries, museums? Or are they outdoorsy, fishing, kayaking, canoeing, riding the rapids, hunters? These are things you need to know.

For women it might be social clubs, charities, art galleries, museums, book clubs, crocheting, knitting, needlepoint, cooking/baking, hiking, sports, or something more adventurous?

What is your character's flaw? All good characters have a flaw. Nail-biting, a certain beer or other alcoholic beverage, a nervous tick, hot temper, runs headlong into trouble without considering the consequences or do they have an independent streak? Do not confuse brand name whiskey such as, Jack Daniels, for bourbon. They are two different beverages. Are they an alcoholic? Substance abuser? Do they smoke or vape? Are they too trusting? Skeptical and suspicious of everything? Do they have a backstory? Does it get in the way?

Where do they live? A bull-riding cowboy most likely lives on a ranch, not some high-rise penthouse in Dallas. He's probably a small-town guy where he is well-known by the locals.

I'll give you a sample from my book *Target of Vengeance:*

Maggie Parsons smiled as she walked down the hall. Her chestnut hair was pulled up into a bun on the top of her head and the beige linen suit outlined her lithe figure. The only sound was the echo of her heels tapping the floor. She had waited a long time to become an elementary principal. Her first job took her back to her own elementary school. How small it seemed now. It seemed so large when she was a child.

The center of the building was two stories high. It had a wing off either end. The offices had been moved to the south end of the building so people, who entered the main doors would enter the main office area. With the way things were today, you wanted to be sure you knew who was in your building at all times. The best way to do it was to have people sign-in at the main office and lock all the other doors during the school day.

Maggie hated the fact children had to be locked up to be safe. Schools should just be safe. Parents should never have to worry about their children when they were at school. Times, like everything else in life, change and the world today made schools targets.

You have an idea what Maggie looks like. You know she has a job as an elementary school principal. You also know it's her first job in this capacity. What else do you know about her? You have the three opening paragraphs; do you want to read more? Why or why not? This book is a suspense novel.

Now comes the time to interview your character.

***Your assignment is:** Go into the Warriors group and introduce your character. Just a couple of lines. Someone else from the group will ask you a question about your character. You answer as if you are your character. The person asking questions should ask a follow-up question or two. You are NOT looking for the entire plot line. You are trying to get to know the character.

No two people will be alike. Some will write gritty scenes, horror writers are writing gruesome images, historical will be fiction based on fact, romance may be love scenes (please NO erotica). Mystery/crime/thriller/suspense will have their plot twists, and red herrings. Some will be more police procedural, others will be court room centered, and there will be those that are time sensitive, (find a cure for a virus, stop a terror attack, rescue hostages), all will find a way to capture their readers.

I will tolerate no trashing of anyone's work EVER.

If you find a character you don't like, skip that one. More than one or two skips is not acceptable. You are supposed to be learning from this how to create a three-dimensional character, someone I might meet on the street.

Get busy on your assignment.

Character name _____

Introduce them in two sentences.

_____

_____

_____

_____

Chapter 8: Following Your Blueprint

Earlier you did an event line for your story. You laid out some things which are going to happen in an order you wanted them to happen. Go back it and read your story so far. You are NOT looking for mistakes. This is NOT where you edit. This is where you make sure you are on track.

1) Have your events changed as the situation changed? Did some extra events get added?

2) How is your planned word count coming?

3) Where are you in your writing?

Please tell me you have something started. If not, figure out what is holding you back. Ask your accountability partner for help. Ask the Warriors for help.

All good writing has a main plot. I had an author write 277 pages with no plot. I'm not sure how it happened because she had a good premise. Along with your plot there are subplots. This is how you get into your character's mind. You learn what makes them tick.

1) What does your protagonist want out of this?

_____

Look at it from the character's point of view. You might learn something about them.

"Bad guys" aren't all bad. They have human sides, too. They have flaws which sometimes hinder them.

2) Are they quick to fly off the handle? _____

3) Are they short term planners who can't see the big picture?

_____

4) Are they a low-life person or a high-level crook? _____

5) Do they love dogs? Children? Cats?

_____

6) Are they fond of the elderly? _____

7) Are they loners or do they have friends to hang-out with?

_____

Every layer you build into your characters makes them richer, more believable, and much more memorable. In *Crossing the Line*, my main antagonist is despicable. She has no redeeming qualities. My readers hate her. She has done awful things. Let me introduce you to her as my readers first meet her. Macy McVannel and Tom Maxwell are investigating why a young girl attempted suicide. They have been led to Chelsie Patton. This is their first meeting:

The secretary handed Tom the file and he returned to the inner office. He sat down and flipped through it. "Well, Chelsie, you look like an intelligent young lady," he said pretending to look at her grades and test scores. He handed the file to me.

"What do you know about it?" she asked her attitude saying more than her words. She was looking down at Tom or at least trying to.

I looked at Chelsie over the top of her file, "I know from your file your grades are decent, you are involved in extracurricular activities, and appear to be on the fast track to the college of your choice. What I've learned from these few pages is, your attitude is going to trip you up."

She glared at me as if her stare would make me go away. *This was the girl of my nightmares, five foot seven, designer clothing, manicured nails, determined to get whatever she wanted no matter who stood in her way.* Michelle was a casualty on Chelsie's road to the boy of her dreams. I also knew Chelsie didn't do her own dirty work she found someone to do it for her. Someone else took the photo. *That* someone would say nothing unless it would keep Chelsie from getting into trouble. We were going to have a battle on our hands.

The door slammed open, Mr. and Mrs. Patton shoved in followed by what I assumed was their lawyer. Mrs. Patton embraced her daughter, "Honey, are you okay? Did these people question you?"

Chelsie dissolved into tears, "Mom, they have been trying to intimidate me." She hugged her mother to show her fears.

Mr. Patton scanned the scene and turned to Tom, "I gave strict instructions my daughter was not to be questioned until I arrived."

Tom stood, "Your daughter has not been questioned other than asking her name and she didn't give it to us. Please, have a seat."

Reluctantly, Mr. Patton took a seat on the other side of his daughter, the lawyer next to him.

Tom remained standing. He began introductions, "I'm Detective Tom Maxwell. This is my partner, Detective Sgt. Macy McVannel. We're looking into some bullying here at the high school for the past couple of days." Tom handed the photo to Mr. Patton who handed it to his lawyer. Mrs. Patton continued to hold their daughter.

"It has come to our attention," I started, "this photo was mass emailed to students from your daughter's computer at home."

"Preposterous!" Mr. Patton shouted.

"Sir, please let Detective McVannel finish," Tom interrupted.

"Out technicians have been working on school computers all morning to find out where the photo came from. They have traced it back to your daughter's home computer. We're trying to track who sent it to her. We need to know why she sent out a mass mailing to five hundred students here at the school."

"There is no way my daughter sent this out." Mr. Patton was red faced as he turned to his daughter, "Tell them, Chelsie, let's get this nonsense cleared up."

Chelsie turned tear-stained eyes to her father, "Daddy, I don't know anything about this photo."

"There you have it. Someone is trying to frame my daughter. She is the victim here." He stood, "We're done. Let's go home."

"Not so fast," I also stood. "We're just beginning this investigation and your daughter is the key. She is either part of the problem or a witness. Until she answers our questions, no one is leaving. *Now*, sit back down and be quiet, Mr. Patton."

Mr. Patton's lawyer tapped his arm and he sat back down. Chelsie looked at her father dumbfounded.

I took my seat and looked at Chelsie, "Now, Young Lady, I need some honest answers from you. Why did you send out the photo?"

She looked at me defiantly, "I did *not* send out that stupid photo."

"Your first lie, Chelsie, we have documentation from the computer techs, and I have a cell phone you sent it to. In fact, I sent you a message from the cell phone to come to the office, and you came." I was very calm as I talked to her. Now, why did you send the photo?"

"The bitch was trying to steal my boyfriend," she spat out the words.

Her mother gasped, "Chelsie."

"Enough," her father said.

"Like this shocks you," the chip on her shoulder seemed to grow. "She'd been warned to back off."

"Who warned her?" Tom asked quietly.

"My friends all told her Matt was my man. She didn't listen and kept making dates with him. I don't know why she had to throw herself at him. He's not interested in her." Chelsie's petty jealousy showed through.

"So, you thought taking an unauthorized photo and sending it out would stop it?" I was incredulous to think she would carry jealousy this far.

"I didn't take the photo; it was one of my friends. I knew it would put the slut in her place. I hear the reason they moved is because she had a reputation for doing all the guys and male teachers at her old school." She tossed her hair as if she were justified in driving the girl to attempt suicide.

"Your information couldn't be more wrong. She moved here because her father died and they came home to her mother's family, to rebuild a life," I said succinctly. "You set out to destroy a young girl, who lost her father over a boy. Who made you judge and jury?"

Chelsie gasped, "It's not true. I heard it from someone reliable."

"It *is* true. Michelle lost her father a few months ago. Her mom was from Rivers Edge and decided to move home after their loss. She sold their home and all their belongings to come here and start over. You may have taken the chance from both of them."

"I didn't make her take the stupid pills. She took them on her own." Chelsie was still in defiant mode.

"You taunted her, threw her clothing in the shower, made sure her lunches were knocked to the floor, her books knocked out of her arms in the hallway, and papers were snatched up to be thrown away. Still she managed to get all As but *this* was uncalled for. I want to know from you who took the photo and I want to know *NOW!*" I said, leaning across the table toward her.

"I did none of those things. I never even talked to the bit…Michelle," she glared at Tom. "I don't know who sent me the photo."

"Did it come to your computer or your cell phone?" I asked calmly.

"It came to my computer. I don't know who sent it," she said, pouting.

There was more to this discussion but I will end it here.

1) What are your opinions of Chelsie?

___

2) Her parents? ___

3) How do you feel about the situation as it is unfolding?

___

4) Do you see yourself as someone who would be friends with Chelsie? Why or why not?_____

_____

Many of you as you read this had a picture of Chelsie in your mind. She is a tormentor from your youth. Someone you would love to forget or better yet would like to see today, in order to see just where she got in the world after making your life miserable.

When writing your villains, remember they must be believable. Chelsie is no one person. She is parts of several young women who passed through my life as a teacher. None of the young ladies I knew were as bad as what Chelsie is in this novel. They all had parts of her personality. I rarely base my characters on people I know. I may pick some of their traits but, when it comes to my characters, they are truly my imagination.

Several times while writing *Crossing the Line,* I found myself getting up and walking away from my writing. I wanted her behind bars and for someone to lose the key. But I had to be true to my characters. Tom Maxwell and Macy McVannel first came on the scene in *Rivers Edge* where you meet them on a cold case. They appear in the Macy McVannel series in *Sanctuary*, which is book three in the series and appear in *Something Borrowed, Something Blue* which released in March 2021.

Macy's flaw in this book is dealing with teenagers who have crossed the line in their bullying and have committed crimes. Their attitudes, their beliefs, and just being teens, make her doubt herself.

*Your assignment: is to figure out the subplot or plots in your story. Both the protagonist and antagonist have something going on. How do they resolve it by the end of the story? Do they resolve it? Make sure you are getting in your word count. Kudos if you are on a roll and over writing your set word count.

Chapter 9: Finding Your Courage

At this point, you should have some direction for your story/novel. Now, you need to be sitting at your computer or have your notebook in front of you. You are staring at a blank page asking yourself, *Can I do this? Am I good enough? Will I be a success? Will I fail? Will people even read what I write?* **STOP!!!**

The only failure is if you never try if you never finish what you have started. If you never try, you will never know if you are any good. You will never know if you can be a success. You will never know if you can complete a story/novel. You will never give people a chance to read your work and know if they like it.

NOW, is the time to let yourself go. Stop staring at the paper. Pick up your pen or pencil, sit at your computer and start writing about those characters you have created. Put them in situations where they must make decisions and then deal with the results of those decisions. Let them play on the paper in front of you.

If you find yourself worried about dialogue, go to your local coffee shop for an hour. Watch the people around you. How are they reacting to the people they are with? Are they angry, animated, casual, disinterested? What are their mannerisms? Do they talk with their hands? Are they actively listening or are they on their phones? If you can't hear their conversations, imagine them.

This is your rough draft, don't get hung up on spelling or punctuation. Just get the words down. Errors can be fixed in editing. Tell your story. Live in the moment with your characters. Allow them to be your guide, set the mood, do their thing. In the end, you will thank them for their input.

Your goal is to write 250 words a day. The idea is to tell your story until there is nothing left to tell. When all the goals have been reached, your characters have grown and adapted to the circumstances and all situations have some conclusion.

- Have they changed or grown?
- Is there a satisfactory ending?
- Are all the questions answered?

Don't let your ending be too abrupt. No questions should be unanswered and make sure everything is tied together. Worry about fine tuning it in edits. You can add and take away in edits. This is the rough draft. Be a storyteller. Get the story written.

You can take out the overused words, misspellings, punctuation, and grammar when it is done. It *must* be written first. Look for any word you use multiple times; so, also, but, since make sure you don't have more than one hundred of these words in a 50,000-word book.

My first novel, *Secrets*, was written in twenty-one days. Was it ready to submit? Not even close. It was completed in November 2005. It was not published until March 2006. I spent time making changes, making sure I had everything as close to perfect as I could. I had it edited by three different people. Finally, I submitted it. Now, it's been edited once again and has come out in its second edition. It was nominated for an Author Elite Award in 2019. No, I didn't make the top ten. Nor did I win. It was an honor to be nominated.

What happened when people other than my family read it? They asked if there was going to be a sequel. It was written as a stand-alone. It had an epilogue, an explanation of where the characters were five years in the future. I had to start thinking about a second book. This is how you get your start. You cannot stand on one book alone. Your readers won't let you.

You sit with paper and pen or at your computer and you write. You tell a story compelling enough to keep your readers turning the pages, because you made it believable. Create characters your readers will love and want to know more about. Make your villains human. They may be despicable, even hated, but above all, they are human even serial killers were kid once.

Characters should be as real to your reader as someone they might meet on the street. They might even consider your characters to be neighbors.

What are you waiting for? _____

Inspiration? _____

A muse? _____

Something magical to happen? _____

You will die with no story written if you are waiting for any of the three above.

This is your invitation to get started. Tell your story. Start writing and get the words out of your head and onto paper. Become the writer you have dreamed of being.

I am waiting to read your first words. I want to know the story you will write. I want to be able to share it with my readers and friends, when it is published. Because I believe when it is written and edited it will be published.

Just sit down and start. You never know what magic might take place. You *are* the inspiration and the magic. You don't need a muse.

_____
_____
_____
_____

Part 4: Finishing Touches

Chapter 10: The Building is Complete

By this time, you should be finishing up your story/novel. You are ready to start looking at it critically. Take a deep breath. Treat yourself to a fancy dinner. Take a friend, spouse, or your significant other. Revel in the completion of your work. Pat yourself on the back. You've come a long way from the opening pages of this book. You have written your own book.

We know it's not ready for the publisher. There is still work to be done. This is a **huge** accomplishment. Because you now know you can write a book. You have done it. See, one obstacle overcome.

All you need to do is walk away from it for a couple of days. Just let it rest in your computer or notebook. Do something you have neglected. Spend some time walking in the woods, golfing, whatever it is you do just to relax.

Once you have done the above, then reread what you have written. You are reading to enjoy the story. You **are** looking for flow and interest, making sure your characters have not stepped out of the story and into another one. Is there something puzzling in what you're reading? Make a note to go back and fix it when you are done reading.

When you have completed your read through, walk away for at least a week. Work on something totally different. Maybe consider starting a second book. Were you writing a series? Now would be a good time to start a new event line. Think of how you will fit your existing characters on this new event line. Are you adding villains? Are you just adding new adventures? How is this connecting to your first novel? How is it different from the first novel?

Some series are written as stand-alone books. John Gilstrap's Jonathan Graves series are only connected by the main characters. Each book is a stand-alone. Once you read one you are done with it. It is complete. Lee Child's Reacher is done the same way. I have a writer friend, doing a seven-book series around a young magician in the 1200s. Each book shows him growing and aging. Each book builds on the previous book. Nora Roberts writes trilogies each book is a part of the whole. Consider which you are writing if you are planning a series.

My Macy McVannel series was originally planned as a trilogy. Each book in the series was intended to be a stand-alone book. Most of my main cast grows or changes in some way. Some things have carried over from one book to the next. It has been exciting to watch it develop. It is now a four-book series with two spin-offs already in print. It will be done at the end of the fourth book except for a couple of already planned spin-offs. At some point in the future, I may even resurrect her for more adventures. For now, she is done.

Each book you write will give you more confidence. It will help develop the writer you will become. The difference between my first novel and the one I am working on is a world of difference. I have gone from a small town to a large city, From murder to something sinister on a larger scale. One which will garner headlines and rock the city with its long reaching implications.

With every book I ask the hard questions: the ones which will make people think.

- Could this happen here?
- Is this what happens when we do something out of the ordinary?

I have chosen tough topics, aside from murder and cold cases, I have written about bullying, spousal and child abuse, stalking, kidnapping and sex trafficking. I try to put a real life, in your neighborhood spin on everyday headlines and issues. Does it mean I am perfect? *Not* by a long shot. I have won an award. I have been nominated for an award. My books sell internationally.

That's all well and good. It looks nice on a bio yet does **not** define me as a writer. My writing defines me. It's who I am and what I do.

Your writing will define you. It will tell people who you are and what you do. There is a little bit of you in everything you write. Those readers, who know you well, will pick out things knowing it is you.

When you can look people in the eye and say: *I am a Writer.* You have gained the confidence you need to keep producing stories and books.

Finally, when the invitation comes to speak to a reading circle. book club, or at a library about your books, you have earned the right to do so. You have the books to back up what you say about yourself. Make sure you take some to sell and sign.

Once you have fixed whatever you needed to correct in your manuscript, it is time to find some beta readers. These are the people who will read your book and give you a one- or two-line blurb which can be put into your book as an endorsement. You will need about six to ten with a variety of people with different backgrounds. You will tell them up front this is **not** an edited version. They are **NOT** reading to correct it. They are reading for enjoyment. Each of them will get a free, signed copy of your book when it is released. Be nice to your readers. You may want them for a second book.

Create a private Facebook page for them. Let them ask questions, discuss the book, and make comments. They will have questions. Some are:

1. Should we tell you about spelling errors? Not necessary, I have an editor working on those.

2. Can I let my wife/husband/partner read it? This is entirely up to your discretion. Know if you tell them, no, they will probably do it anyway. My opinion is the more the merrier,

however the original person is the only one who gets a free book. We do not want it passed to everyone they know.

3. Can I ask a question if I am confused? By all means. You don't want your readers confused.

4. What if they think the main character did something out of character? You want to know this.

Chapter 11: Who Are You?

This may sound like a strange question, it's not. Now is the time to think about what you want your readers to know about you. You need to write your bio. This will go in the back of your book with a head shot. No, I did not say mug shot. This should be a photo taken by a professional. Think about how you want your readers to see you. Your bio should be around 200 words.

Whoa, that's not much. No, it isn't. Tell them something about who you are.

1. What brought you to the writing field?

2. Why this book?

3. Maybe some of your hobbies.

4. The state you live in (country or province if you do not live in the United States). You are not ready to have readers banging on your front door.

5. How do they contact you?

6. Are you on Facebook, Twitter, Instagram, LinkedIn, or any other social media?

7. Do you have a website?

8. Can they contact you by email? Please tell me you have set up an author page on Facebook. You do not want fans all over your personal page. You can invite friends to your author page.

This is your time to shine. Here's my bio:

> Retired teacher Rebecka Vigus is an author, speaker, and coach.
>
> Ms. Vigus has been writing since she was ten when a teacher told her, with her imagination he would see her in books one day. She believed him and started writing then.

While teaching, she published the second edition of her poetry book and has gone on to write fifteen more books.

She loves spending time with family and friends. She uses her leisure time to read, crochet, swim, hike, and travel. She lives in her forever home in Nancy, Kentucky amid the wildlife and horses.

You can find her:

Her website: https://www.rebeckavigus.com

LinkedIn: https://www.linkedin.com/in/rebecka-vigus-6b638117/

Facebook: https://www.facebook.com/RebeckaVigusTheWriterWhisperer

YouTube: https://www.youtube.com/channel/UC_bW3aeg9SUM0d3y0bxZv9w

This one is less than 200 words. I had one at one time at 210 words. You don't have to say much, just give some facts. They will Google you to find your presence. My writing blog is a link on my website, so I don't include it. I have a personal blog. If readers find it, it's fine with me. This bio gets used for my books and my coaching. It changes a bit every year as I have to update the number of books I have written.

I went to a writing conference and the first breakout speaker was gentleman named, Steve Brewer. His opening statement was:

"I am Steve Brewer the most prolific writer you have never read."

At the time, he had twenty-seven books published. I have two of them. He tends to write comic mystery. His main character's name is Elvis Cole. I have since heard he has one of his books being made into a movie

Think about how you want readers to see you. Not just your photo, but you as a writer. For your photo, have them taken professionally. If you know someone who is a photographer and will give you a good price on a sitting, take them up on it. It cost me $50 for my first professional sitting and the photographer was a former student just starting out. My second sitting cost me a bundle at J C Penney and I had a coupon for $50 off. I wasn't too thrilled with the results either. My third sitting was a nightmare, but it was only $50. My latest sitting was done for my branding as a coach. My brand colors are red with purple accents. I wanted them taken in casual office and casual. They cost me a couple hundred but were stunning.

Figure out your power color. Have business and casual poses taken. Some will be for advertising. One will be for the back of your book and your media kit. Some will be for speaking engagements. Find your brand colors you are comfortable with and make you feel confident.

If you don't have a website, find someone to do one for you. Think about how you want it to look. You will use your brand colors here. You can try fiverr.com to find someone to do a website for you. If you know someone who does websites, make sure they will work with you to get what you want.

Write your bio. Put it away. After a week, take it out and tweak it. Fix the spelling errors. Add or subtract from it. Make it tell the world who you are.

Bio:

_____

_____

_____

_____

_____

_____

_____

_____

_____

_____

_____

Connect with me:

Facebook:

LinkedIn:

Twitter:

Whatsapp:

Instagram:

Website:

Chapter 12: Inspecting for Errors

The flare pens I told you would be needed should be pulled out and readied. Now is the time to pick one out. Not yellow. You are going to read through your manuscript. Every time you find a misspelled word or other error, you will underline it with your pen. Put an X at the top right corner of the page.

The X tells you there is at least one error on the page. If you have misplaced or omitted punctuation, put it in and mark the page so you will know you have to fix it in the computer. Pages which are error free, do **NOT** put an X on. When you are editing in the computer, you can skip these pages.

When you have gone through the entire manuscript and fixed the errors you need to print off two copies. Then find two trusted friends who know something about grammar and ask if they will take two weeks (You MUST give them a deadline) and read through it and make corrections or suggestions. Give each of them a different color pen than the one you used and the one they will use (each of them gets a different color so no two are the same). Tell them to put an X in the top right-hand corner of every page where they found something to be fixed. If it is not convenient for them to complete it two weeks, please find someone else. **Do Not** touch your manuscript for the two weeks while you wait. Write anything else but leave the manuscript alone.

When you get the manuscripts back, collate them so you have page one and page one. It will make doing corrections go smoother. Now sit at the computer. Make the corrections from the first page one and put it aside. Make any corrections from the second page one. Be sure to read any comments which have been made. Do this through the entire manuscript. Put the names of your two editors on your list of people to get free books.

After you have completed these edits, you should be ready to hand it off to a professional editor. Find an editor you can work with. You will want to work with them on future books. Find out if they are doing line editing, mechanical editing, and/or content editing. Ideally, they will do all three. Find someone who fits into your budget.

The going rate for proofreading is $3/page. It is $4/page for copy editing which is grammar and spelling. Then, $7-$8/page for content editing or line editing. If you get a good editor who does both copy and line editing, it could cost you between $11-$12/page. So, be sure you know the what the editor does as well as what is being charged. A line editor will cost you between $1400-$1600. Your total would be somewhere between $2200 and $2600. Shop around. If you find one that does both, you might get away with $9-$10/page and a cost of $1800-$2000.

There are also editors who charge by the word. They start at roughly $0.04 a word. A 50,000-word book would be about $2000. Look at your options. Talk to editors. Find one you can afford and work with.

Now you've found an editor and you have turned over your manuscript.

What do you do?

Look for a publisher.

Work on a new book.

Think about how you want to launch your book.

What is your platform? Work on it, because your platform is **not**: "Hey, I've written a book. Please buy it."

You can borrow a platform.

What is your topic?

Is it something which already has a platform and people talking about it? If so, borrow it. For *Crossing the Line,* the topic is bullying. There are many platforms about bullying you can borrow.

What do you want people to take away from your book besides a good read?

What do you want them talking about?

In my book, *Crossing the Line,* the underlying theme is bullying and the way it affects others. It also pointed out how bullying can be illegal. Bullying is a topic everyone gives lip service to however: no one has come up with a solution for preventing it. With social media, bullying has gone from local to national.

- What does your book say?
- Who does your book serve?

Part 5: Up for Sale

Chapter 13: Open House

You have your manuscript back. You've made all the corrections your editor found. The next step is to find an agent and/or a publisher.

There are several ways for you to do to this. First, go to the library. Find *The Writers Market* for the current year. Look for your genre. Read everything you can find on any publishers you are interested in. If they are asking you for money and plan to take a percentage of your royalties, they are a vanity press…run and run fast. Make a list of the publishers you are interested in. Make a note as to whether or not they require an agent. Then, use a computer and look up https://www.sfwa.org/other-resources/for-authors/writer-beware/ This organization will tell you if the publisher you chose is a good or bad choice. They have been doing this since 1998. They also do agents. It is always better to know what you are getting into.

Now go to the first publisher on your list and enter their website. Look for submissions. Read all the guidelines carefully.

What chapters are they looking for?

Are they only looking for the first 5,000 words?

Do not send any more than they request.

Can you send an email submission? You can for most who do not require an agent.

You will need a query letter and a synopsis. Attach the required pages. Send it to the submissions department. Do let them know if you are sending it to other publishers.

What do you put in a query letter?

A short bio of yourself.

A synopsis of your book not more than a single page. Tell them how your book is different from other books in your genre.

Don't forget to put in your contact information. If you snail mailed your query, make sure you have included a self-addressed, stamped envelope if you want it back.

Not sure what sets you apart?

Look at some books in your genre.

Why is your book different?

Seriously, how many ways can you murder someone? In *Secrets*, the murder was not only about the deceased, but also the impact it had on a small town and the things you learn about your community when you are forced to look at everyone as suspects. We all think we know someone's secrets until we find out we don't.

Getting results from your submissions can take six to eight weeks. Some will take even less time. You are still writing, working on your book launch, talking to people about the significance of your book. Writing is what you need to be doing. If your book is a series, you had better have a start on the next one. The publisher will ask you about it.

Keep yourself writing. The next idea is around the corner. The author of the *Chicken Soup for the Soul* books had 147 rejections prior to being accepted. They are bestsellers now in many formats.

Keep sending out your submissions and preparing for your launch.

Chapter 14: Final Offer

You have an offer from a publisher. It is either a traditional publisher, a hybrid publisher, or a small press. The traditional publisher may pay you a small advance. You are an unknown so will not get a huge advance. They are buying your book and expect to make money from this. Your royalty will be about 20%. It works like this; your book is priced at $14.95 in paperback form. It sells and the publisher pays you 20% which is $2.99. In order for you to make money, you will need to sell 2,000 books to make $5,980. That's not a career change. Those are just from bookstore and online sales.

If you go with a small press, you might get 60%-65% of your royalties. They are working with you and helping you brand yourself. They are investing time and money in you. They want both of you to make money. The 60 to 65% they pay you is not from your cover price. It is from the price someone pays for your book. If your book is purchased by Amazon, Barnes & Noble or any other bookstore they generally get a 30-45% discount on the purchase price. Your 60-65% commission comes after that discount. Cost to publish your book is $5.15. Amazon gets 40% for a discount and only pays $3.09. You get 60% of the $3.09 which is $1.85. If you sell 2,000 you get $3,708. You still cannot quit your day job.

A hybrid publisher charges you to publish your book but keeps none of your royalties. You would need an IngramSpark account and a Draft2Digital account. The publisher generally does your interior and cover design. Upfront costs vary from hybrid-to-hybrid publisher. You need ISBNs which you will buy from your publisher and there is the cost of the interior and cover. Depending on who you use you are looking at anywhere from $525-$1200. Remember, you are keeping 100% of your royalties, which is really about 60%. Better than the 20% offered by traditional publishers or the 60% small presses offer.

You can also consider self-publishing. Go to fiverr.com and find someone to create a logo you can put on the back of your books. Then find someone to do the interior and cover art. I recommend www.ebookorprint.com. They have done a couple of books for me. You want paperback covers, eBook covers, audiobook covers, and hard covers. Register at Bowker.com and buy some ISBNs. Get an account with IngramSpark.com and draft2digital.com. IngramSpark will prepare and print your hard cover and paperback books and they have worldwide distribution. Amazon does not. They are only allowed to sell in countries where they have warehouses. They do not have warehouses in Eastern Europe or Asia.

Draft2digital is where you will upload your eBooks. They have a wide distribution which includes libraries. Audiobooks will go through Audible which I believe is ACX.

Upload your completed books and set a date for sale. With IngramSpark set the date two weeks after you put it on pre-sale. Put the pre-sale link on your website and make it payable through the website.

If your book is a series, you want a couple of chapters from the next book in the back of your book with a projected sale date. Give them a season and a year. Don't make them wait forever. For example: You plan the next book to be out in April of the following year. Your projected date would be Spring, 2023. In case, something happens and it doesn't make it out until May. You could conceivably launch a book every quarter depending on how fast you write.

Some of you will have story starts everywhere. This is a good thing. Make a list of the stories you want to write. Give them a deadline over the next five years. I have a five-year plan through 2029. Yes, I realize that is more than five years. I keep adding and shuffling books. I launched two books in 2020. I had four ready and my publisher dropped me. I launched two books in 2021 and have four more started. My five-year plan got revamped. It gets revamped as one book is launched and a new one moves into the slot.

If you were pleased with whomever you chose to do your book interior and covers, please let them know and consider working with them on your next books to build your brand, so your covers are recognizable as yours on the bookshelf. It should be a style where the cover draws the readers' eye to your book. No, the covers do not have to look alike.

Each of my book covers is a different color, different background. They represent the story inside. It's what my readers have come to expect from my covers.

If you want to make money, you have done a pre-sale and have ordered those books, signed, and sent them. Now, you need to have your book launch. This is where you host a live event, invite 200 of your closest friends, and get someone to live stream the event. It will cost you a bit of money, but you will be selling books, not just to the folks who come, but also to those who are watching the live stream can order books. You should be able to get your books at a discount from your publisher. The book retails for $14.95 but you should get it for cost of printing, which is anywhere between $5 and $7 each. When you sell them at retail price plus whatever sales tax you have to charge, you get to keep all the money (except the sales tax which you have to pay to your state). Those buying online are also paying shipping. Now, you are making between $7.95-$9.95/book. Income will vary depending on whether people buy paperback or hardcover. You want to give away the ebook or paperback and some Amazon gift cards.

After the launch, you need to start looking for places which will allow you to have a book signing: bookstores, used bookstores, libraries, or grocery stores. Each of these places will want a percentage of your profits for the day. They will run them through their cash register, so you won't have to worry about sales tax. Percentages will run anywhere from 25%-45%. Keep track of each book you sell so you can compare it with the store's tally. You also need this information for inventory.

I went to a bookstore for their Christmas sale. All the stores stayed open until 8:30pm that night. Carolers were going to come to all the stores and sing. The bookstore was dead. I sold one book and left copies of others there on consignment. After her percentage she owed me $10.50. It took me two months to get the check. She could have paid me from her cash register. She sold the bookstore without telling the new owners I had books there on consignment. If any have been sold, I have no idea. Lost money. Make sure you are being paid at the end of the signing if you are in a bookstore. Grocery stores could take 2-3 weeks to send you a check.

Anyone who has a vendor show could offer you a table to sell your books if they are appropriate to their clientele. Table costs vary with events and you would need to be available during the event to sell books. I advise taking someone with you so you can get breaks for bathroom and lunch. Don't plan your lunch at the same time as the event is holding lunch, you will lose sales as some people will buy from you before or after they have lunch.

Offer your books at a bulk discount to book clubs and groups. Once they say yes, tell them you'd be happy to come speak to their group for a fee. Be reasonable. If there are only ten women in the group offer them a 10% -15% discount on the books and see what they will offer to pay you as a speaker. Always ask what a group is offering to pay you as a speaker. Be reasonable if they ask you how much you want. Small groups, $50-$100 large groups, would be more and conferences would be the most. Then sell your books to them after. Those are ways to make extra money.

Do the math, what fits your budget? Do what feels right to you. Don't let some salesperson sell you a bill of goods. Find out which one works best for you.

I have self-published. I have been with a hybrid publisher. I have been with a small press and owned a small press. I go between self-publishing and a hybrid publisher. I once wanted to see my books in Barnes & Noble. It no longer matters if my books are there. Barnes & Noble can order my books for you and they carry them online. I would much rather my books grace the shelves of an independent bookstore where they are most likely to be seen and purchased.

Chapter 15: Sold

You have chosen your publisher and been offered a contract. Read the contract carefully. Find someone who knows something about intellectual property and have them read it. There might be someone at a local community college. If not, try the closest university, otherwise you will be looking for an intellectual attorney. You do not want to be cheated.

Amtrak offered authors a discounted ride on their trains to write. When you read the fine print, they wanted to own the rights to anything you wrote while in this program. I don't think so. I took a James Patterson writing class online and highly recommend it. You could submit what you wrote for the class for a chance to become his next writing partner. Fine print said he would own the rights to what you submitted. I am not giving my work away.

Read the fine print to make sure you are NOT being cheated. Find someone who knows about intellectual property to also read it. I don't care if you have to hire an attorney to do this. It's in your best interests to have someone who knows look at it.

Now you start pushing your book. Start the hype. See if you can get a photo of the cover use it to send to local television and radio stations. Send a copy to the local newspapers. Put it on your author page on Facebook. Get people interested in it. Have them talking about it. This is where you build the momentum for your launch.

As soon as your publisher has a release date, you plan for your pre-orders. Get a link set up where people can order in advance. As soon as you can order copies, do so. Take into consideration the pre-sales as well as the books you are giving to beta readers and first editors as well as how many you might need for the actual launch.

I know a woman who made $50,000 between pre-sales and launch sales. She did a lot of self-promotion. Her book was a memoir. Any book can make this much if you spend time self-promoting it. You have to work at self-promotion.

Hire a publicist, someone who can get you on TV and radio interviews. Sign up for podcasts. Start your own podcast. Write a blog or set up a YouTube channel and start talking about the book. There are hundreds of ways to get yourself known. You want people to know your name and know you have written a book which might change their life. It can be fictional and still change lives by making you think about things in different ways. My books are conversation starters, they get people thinking about different social issues.

Make bookmarks with the book cover on one side and how to reach you on the other. Put one in every book you sell. Have business cards made use a branding photo (a photo of you so people will recognize you) and give your contact information. Books are not a business card. Books are meant to change lives.

Once you have the books in your hands, it's up to you to get them sold. I keep 10 copies of my books on hand all the time. I reorder when I get to five. I sell my books from my website and at book signings. I wear my branding colors when I am signing my books.

Once you have been offered a contract and all parties agree, you can go celebrate! You will be on Amazon as an author, don't forget to set up your author page there. You will be at Barnes and Noble, plus all the other outlets. You will have paperback, hardcover, audiobooks, eBooks, and Mp4 downloads. You are on your way.

Get busy on the second book. You have the tools, the ideas, and the ability to get another book written. When your proof copy arrives in your hand, have someone take your photo with it and add it to the Facebook group. We all want to see your success. Then, read it through carefully. Look for spelling errors, missing punctuation, anything not matching what you wrote. Notify your publisher of any changes immediately. DO NOT wait. Once they are changed, give your publisher the go ahead to print and start promoting get your book.

I am counting on you to get this done and to become the next person I see on the NYT Bestseller list or the USA Today bestseller list.

Don't forget there are contests you can enter to see if your book will win any awards. I am counting on you to go win awards.

Appendices

Appendix A: Recommended Reading

1. The Complete Idiot's Guide to Forensics, by Alan Axelrod and guy Antinozzi, Alpha/Penguin Group, 2007

2. Black's Law Dictionary for those writing crime fiction

3. Bulletproof Book Proposals, by Pam Brodowsky and Eric Neuhaus, Writers Digest Books, 2006. Yes, fiction books should have a proposal.

4. Private Eyes: A Writer's Guide to Private Investigations by Hal Blythe, Charlie Sweet, and John Landroth, Writers Digest Books, 1993

5. The Complete Idiot's Guide to Getting Published, by Sheree Bykofsky and Jennifer Basye Sander, Alpha/Penguin Group,2006

6. The Artist's Way, by Julia Cameron, Jeffery Thatcher/Penguin Press, 2016

7. The Artist's Date Book, by Julia Cameron, Jeffery Thatcher/Penguin Press, 1999

8. The Right to Write, by Julia Cameron, Jeffery Thatcher/Putnam, 1998

9. The Sound of Paper, by Julia Cameron, Jeffery Thatcher/Putnam, 2004

10. The Key: How to Write Damn Good Fiction Using the Power of Myth, by James N. Frey, St. Martin's Press, 2002

11. How to Write a Damn Good Mystery: A Practical Step-by-Step Guide from Inspiration to Manuscript, by James N. Frey, St. Martin's press, 2007

12. How to Write a Damn Good Thriller: A Step-by-Step Guide for Novelists and Screenwriters, by James N. Frey, St. Martin's Press, 2010

13. How to Write a Damn Good Novel: A Step-by-Step No-Nonsense Guide to Dramatic Storytelling, by James N. Frey, St. Martin's Press, 2010

14. How to Write a Damn Good Novel II: Advanced Techniques for Dramatic Storytelling, by James N. Frey, St. Martin's Press, 2011

15. The Fastest Way to Write Your Book, by Dave Haslett, ideas4writers.co.uk, 2005

16. You Can Market Your Book by Carmen Leal, Write Now Publications, 2003

17. Guerrilla Marketing, by Jay Conrad Levinson, Houghton Mifflin Company, 2007

18. Police Procedure and Investigation, by Lee Lofland, Writer's Digest Books, 2007

19. Writing the Break-out Novel: Insider Advice for Taking Your Fiction to the Next Level, by Donald Maass, Writer's Digest Books, 2002 This one also has a workbook

20. The Novelist's Toolkit, by Bob Mayer, Writer's Digest Books, 2003

21. The Write Brain Workbook by Bonnie Neubauer, Writer's Digest Books, 2006

22. Armed and Dangerous: A Writer's Guide to Weapons, by Michael Newton, Writers Digest Books, 1990

23. The War of Art: Break Through the Blocks and Win Your Inner Creative Battles, by Steven Pressfield, Black Irish Entertainment, 2002

24. Do The Work, by Steven Pressfield, Do You Zoom, Inc. 2011

25. The Weekend Novelist, by Robert J. Ray, Dell Publishing, 1994

26. The Writer's Retreat, by Judy Reeves, New World Library, 2005

27. If You Can Talk, You Can Write, by Joel Saltzman, Warner Books, 1993

28. The Complete Idiot's Guide to Self-Publishing, by Jennifer Basye Sander, Alpha/Penguin Group, 2005

29. From Book to Bestseller: An Insider's Guide to Publicizing and Marketing Your Book, by Penny C. Sansevieri, PublishingGold.com, Inc, 2005

30. Make Your Creative Dreams Real: A Plan for Procrastinators, Perfectionists, Busy People and People Who Would Really Rather Sleep All Day, by SARK, Atria Books, 2005

31. Techniques of a Selling Writer, by David V. Swain, University of Oklahoma Press, 1965

32. Cause of Death: A Writer's Guide to Death, Murder and Forensic Medicine, by Keith D. Wilson, MD, Writer's Digest Books, 1992.

33. Guide to Fiction Writing, by Phyllis A. Whitney, The Writer's Inc, 1982

34. Scene of the Crime: A Writer's Guide to Crime Scene Investigation, by Anne Wingate, Ph. D., Writer's Digest Books, 1992

35. The Mini Market Book: Everything You Need to Know to get Published, Including 125 Markets for New Writers, Writer's Digest Books, 2007

Appendix B: Writing Contests

1. The Pushcart Prize: Nominations are accepted from Oct 1-Dec 1 for the following year. Books must be published. Mail (up to 6 nominations) to: Pushcart Press, PO Box 380, Wainscott, NY 11975 There is no fee to enter.

2. https://www.writersdigest.com/wd-competitions/ For this you need to be self-published. I believe there is a $75 entry fee. You will have to go through the list to find the correct contest for your book.

3. http://internationalbookawards.com Deadline for this is April 30, 2023. Please read all their guidelines. The fee is $69/category. If your book could be in more than one category you want to enter it in more than one.

4. http://americanbookfest.com Deadline is October 15th. Please read all their guidelines. Fee is again $69/category.

5. https://www.entertheimaginarium.com/category/imadjinn-awards/ Generally opens submissions in early September and close in February. Please read all guidelines. Awards are given in July. Nominations are to be made by the publisher, the author, or a representative of the publisher. No fee that I can see in their guidelines.

6. https://storymonsters.com This is everything children's books. It has three categories of contests: Story Monster Approved, Royal Dragonfly and Purple Dragonfly. Story Monster Approved Applications Early bird deadline: November 1 $65 Final deadline February 1 $70. Royal Dragonfly: Are accepting for 2023 Early bird deadline August 1, 2023 $65 and the final deadline: October 3, 2023. Purple Dragonfly: Early deadline March 1, 2023 $65 and the final deadline: May 2, 2023.

7. https://www.readerschoiceawards.com They do awards twice a year, spring and autumn. Current deadlines are: July1 to September1 for autumn and October 1 to March 31 for spring. There is no fee unless you are looking for a review.

8. https://www.indieexcellence.com This one is for self-published authors. Fee is $75 and deadline is March 31, 2023. Please read all guidelines.

9. https://indiebookawards.com Books will have be mailed or sent by courier. The fee is $75 for the first title and $60 for additional titles. An application must accompany each entry. Deadline is February 10, 2023

10. https://readersfavorite.com Deadline is April 1, 2023 Fee is $99 for the first book and $65 for any additional books.

11. http://hollywoodbookfest.brinkster.net Late submissions for 2022 were due in August. The fee is $75/entry. Please read the guidelines for submission. Mailed packages must contain a check or a receipt from an online payment and the application plus a copy of the book. I have no knowledge of how reputable this contest is. It is listed as a place for new writers to apply.

This being a pretty good list, note that most of them require an ISBN number for the book you are entering. This is a safeguard for you so your work cannot be stolen. The only one I have no knowledge about is the Hollywood Book Fest. It doesn't mean they are not reputable; it just means I am not familiar with them. You could check it on writerbeware.com to see what they have to say about it.

Appendix C: Job Application

Acknowledgements

Books like many things are not completed in isolation. It takes several people to get them right. I have many people to thank for this book. Cecilia Winslow Tucker and Caitlin Turner who took writing classes from me when I first started coaching and helped me to understand what I was missing in my coaching.

Mackenzie Flohr for writing a foreword to this book. She didn't have to. She took the time to read the book and then write the foreword. Mackenzie is busy writing a screen play for her own books.

Then, to Janice Harris who did the editing for this book. I appreciate her insights and comments. She helped to make this a much better book.

To Kary Oberbrunner who has taught me so much since 2019 and continues to do so with infinite patience.

Finally, to Jerry Reid at ebookorprint.com for the beautiful cover design and setup. This wouldn't have happened without you.

Thank you seems inadequate.

About the Author

Retired teacher Rebecka Vigus is an author, speaker, and coach.

Ms. Vigus has been writing since she was ten when a teacher told her, with her imagination he would see her in books one day. She believed him and started writing then. Her first book was poetry titled *Only a Start.*

While teaching, she published the second edition of her poetry book and has gone on to write fifteen more books.

She loves spending time with family and friends. She uses her leisure time to crochet, swim, hike, and travel. She lives in her forever home in Nancy, Kentucky amid the wildlife, cattle, and horses.

You can find her:

Facebook: https://www.facebook.com/RebeckaVigusTheWriterWhisperer

Website: https://www.rebeckavigus.com

LinkedIn: https://www.linkedin.com/in/rebecka-vigus-6b638117/

YouTube: https://www.youtube.com/channel/UC_bW3aeg9SUM0d3y0bxZv9w

Other Books by Rebecka Vigus

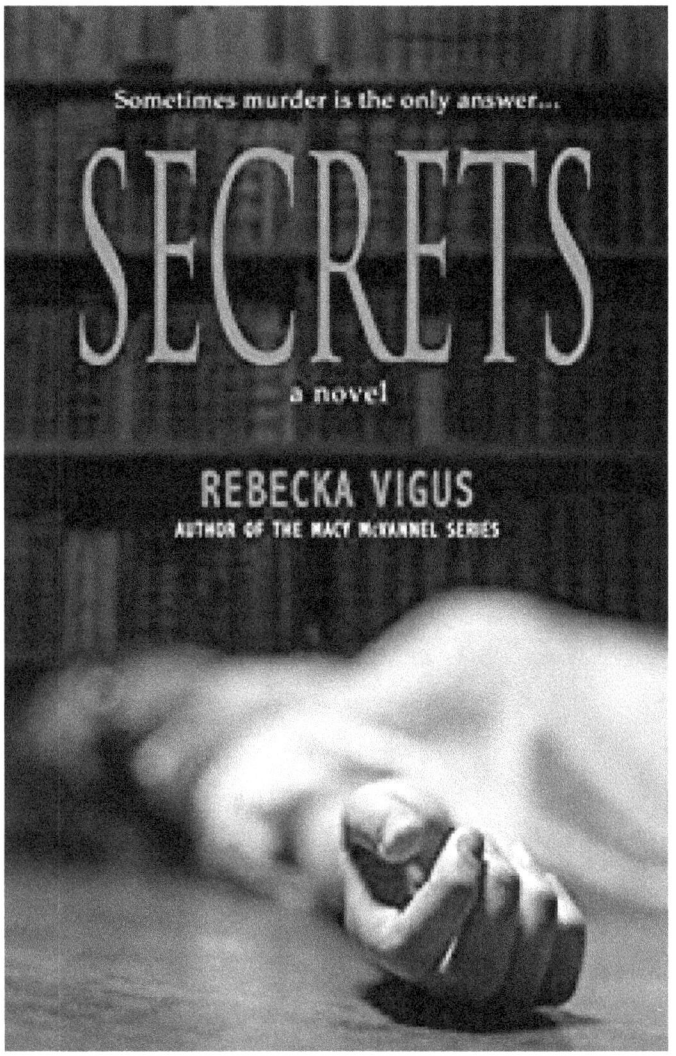

In the small town of Oak Grove the local librarian is murdered. No one can figure out who would want to harm her…or why. Chief of Police, Buck Wise finds himself engulfed in the secrets of his hometown, the mob, and state senators. Can he discover why Miss Emily was murdered and who did it?

https://www.rebeckavigus.com/

Meet Macy McVannel By Rebecka Vigus

Book 1 in the Macy McVannel series

When a sixteen-year-old cold case ends up in the hands of Detective Sergeant Macy McVannel and her partner Detective Tom Maxwell, it's up to them to figure things out. As they dig deeper into the murder of Mrs. Appleton's son, they start running into a problem…their witnesses are turning up dead. Nobody is safe—not even the captain. Forced into hiding, McVannel and Maxwell must apprehend a killer while trying to survive the hidden mysteries of Rivers Edge

https://www.rebeckavigus.com/

Of Moonbeam and Fairies: Collected Tales

by Rebecka Vigus

Let the moonbeams take you where your imagination lives.
A whimsical book of poems and short stories featuring gnomes, fairies, elves, fireflies, leprachauns, and other real and fictitious characters aimed to capture the imagination of youngsters. These imaginary places will entice you to believe what you cannot see.

https://www.rebeckavigus.com/

www.ingramcontent.com/pod-product-compliance
Lightning Source LLC
Chambersburg PA
CBHW081230080526
44587CB00022B/3889